What a Scientist Sees

Dona Herweck Rice

Consultant

Leann Iacuone, M.A.T., NBCT, ATC
Riverside Unified School District

Publishing Credits

Rachelle Cracchiolo, M.S.Ed., *Publisher*
Conni Medina, M.A.Ed., *Managing Editor*
Diana Kenney, M.A.Ed., NBCT, *Senior Editor*
Dona Herweck Rice, *Series Developer*
Robin Erickson, *Multimedia Designer*
Timothy Bradley, *Illustrator*

Image Credits: Cover & p.1 Shutterstock; p.10 67photo / Alamy; p.22 Agencja Fotograficzna Caro / Alamy; p.10 Aurora Photos / Alamy; p.11 Blend Images / Alamy; p.26 David R. Frazier Photolibrary, Inc. / Alamy; p.27 Gabbro / Alamy; pp.28, 29 Grace Le; p.3 Hongqi Zhang / Alamy; p.14 INDEDUC / Alamy; pp.7, 8, 12, 14, 15, 16, 17, 18, 19, 20, 21, 32 iStock; p.25 Kim Karpeles / Alamy; all other images
from Shutterstock.

Library of Congress Cataloging-in-Publication Data

Rice, Dona, author.
What a scientist sees / Dona Herweck Rice.
pages cm
Summary: "How does it work? What does it do? What happens if...? Scientists ask many great questions. Many of these questions lead to more questions. Start by noticing the things around you, and let your curiosity take over!"-- Provided by publisher.
Audience: Grades 4 to 6.
Includes index.
ISBN 978-1-4807-4691-6 (pbk.)
1. Scientists--Juvenile literature. 2. Science--Methodology--Juvenile literature. I. Title.
Q163.R476 2016
500--dc23
2014045214

Teacher Created Materials
5301 Oceanus Drive
Huntington Beach, CA 92649-1030
http://www.tcmpub.com

ISBN 978-1-4807-4691-6

Printed in China
Nordica.082019.CA21901024

Table of Contents

Tricky Business

As soon as you finish reading this sentence, close this book for about one minute and try to remember everything you can about the picture on the right.

How did you do? How much did you recall? If you remembered a lot, then congratulations! You've got a knack for noticing details.

So now, take a good look at the picture. Observe it closely. What objects are in the picture? Describe them. What colors and shapes are the objects? How tall are they, and how close are they to one another? What are the people doing? Are people paying attention to one another? How do people seem to be feeling? Are they happy, sad, angry, or surprised? Do you see anything funny?

All right, now here's the most important question of all. Who in the world cares about all these details?

A scientist does, that's who.

Doctors, lawyers, artists, engineers, housekeepers, musicians, actors, singers, hair stylists, chefs, athletes, directors, teachers, and accountants all need to pay attention to details. Learning to pay attention will help you in any job!

A scientist notices EVERYTHING! Why? Because a scientist knows that every detail matters.

Let's say a scientist is working with two **chemicals**. When they are mixed together in **equal** parts, a puff of periwinkle blue smoke shoots into the air. This happens every time. But one day, the scientist mixes two equal chemical parts, and this time, the blue is cerulean (suh-ROO-lee-uhn). *That's odd*, thinks the scientist. He double-checks his notes. *Yes, the blue smoke is ALWAYS periwinkle*, he confirms. So, why cerulean this time? Something has to be different. There's a detail, even a small one, that made the difference. A good scientist needs to know why, and our scientist is a good one.

Try It!

How many shades of blue can you make by mixing paint? Find out by mixing blue paint with different amounts of black, or white, or dabs of yellow or red. Keep a record of the mixtures you create.

Through careful **observation**, the scientist discovers something important. He dropped a piece of his tuna-fish sandwich into the chemicals! Well, no wonder things were different. Next time, there's no eating in the laboratory!

Scientific Method

Before going any further, it's important that you understand something. You need to know the process every good scientist uses when **conducting** experiments. Scientists follow the **scientific method**. This process was developed by scientists to help them do the work they need to do. Every scientist uses this method in his or her investigations. Without it, there really isn't much purpose to their work! Their work would just be random. And *random* does not make for good science.

In case you don't know the scientific method, here it is. And if you do know the method, read this anyway. A refresher course will be good for you!

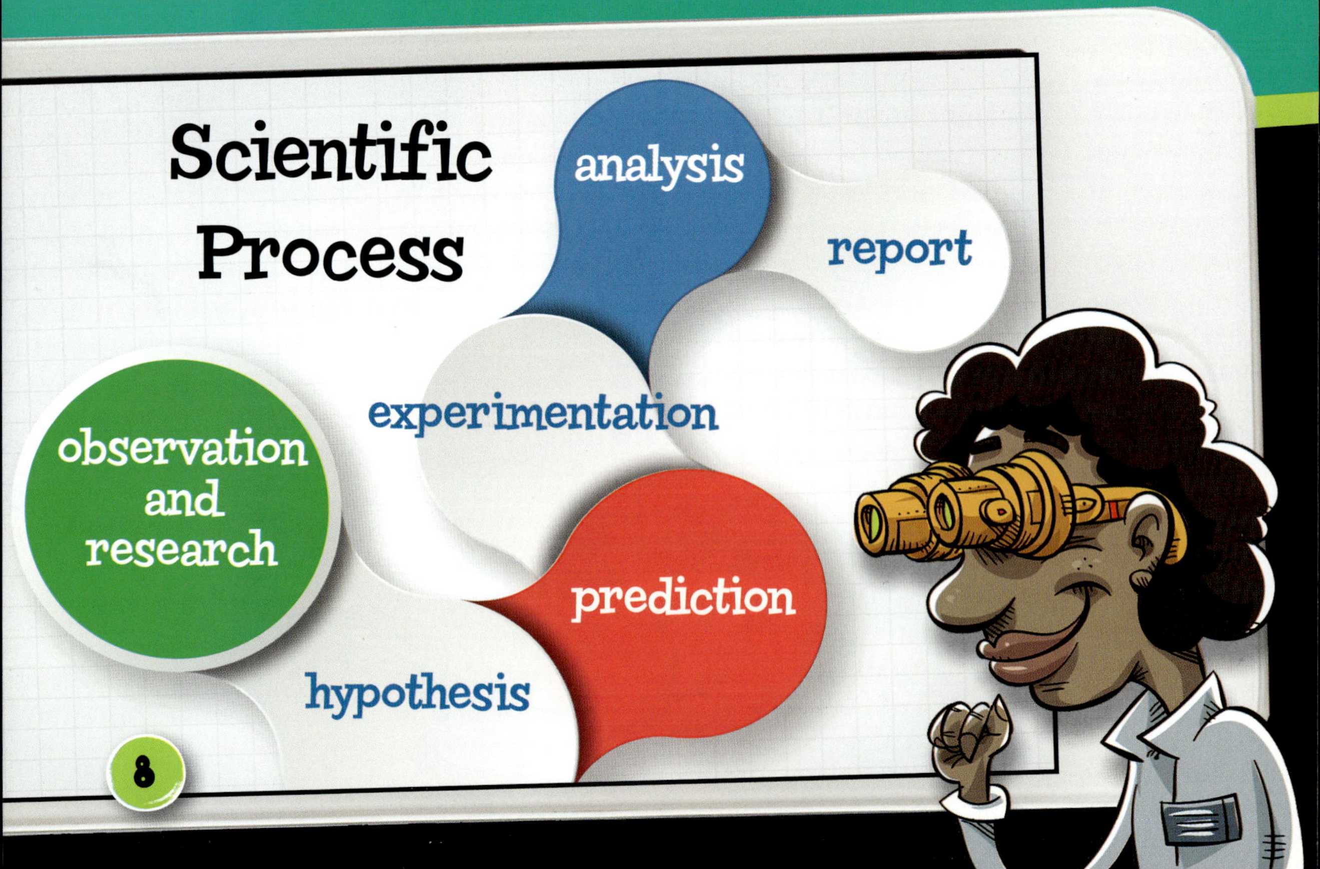

The basic scientific method can be listed in six simple steps: observation and **research**, **hypothesis**, **prediction**, experimentation, analysis, and report.

A scientist begins any good work by learning what there is to know about a topic. She learns by researching the work of other scientists and by observing. From this, she forms a hypothesis. That's something a scientist assumes from the known information. It's like a guess, but it's a guess with a lot of solid information behind it. Maybe it's *Tuna fish added to chemicals A and B makes cerulean blue smoke*.

See, Think, Ask

Scientists keep their eyes open because they never know when they might find a new scientific mystery or come up with a new question to investigate. Here are just a few of the questions scientists have asked.

- Why do dogs have wet noses?
- Which foods are safe to eat?
- What causes muscle cramps?
- How are rats related to raccoons?

So, how does a scientist know if the hypothesis is **valid**? She has to test it. And to test it, she needs to make a good prediction. The scientist predicts something about the hypothesis. Then, she tests her prediction. For example, *I predict the two chemicals mixed in equal parts with no tuna fish will create periwinkle blue smoke.*

This is where things get really fun. It's time to experiment! A scientist uses experiments to see if a hypothesis is true or false. Experiments are tests. A scientist repeats a test many times to be sure the results are the same. That's the only way a hypothesis can be proven.

Compare results with hypothesis.

Reproducing Your Results

When designing an experiment, it's important to come up with a test that can be done again and again. Take careful notes of what steps you took so someone else can take the exact same steps and see if the result is exactly the same. This is the best way to test a hypothesis.

When the experiments are complete, the scientist **analyzes** the results. She determines if the hypothesis is proven or not. She then accepts or rejects the hypothesis.

At long last, the scientist can tell the world about her work. Now, she is ready to report her findings. In this way, other scientists can check her work and do their own work based on hers.

Make It Simple

Some questions can be so complicated that it's difficult to know when you're seeing the answer. Scientists make their experiments as simple as possible and try to tease out details so there can be no doubt what the answer is.

Observe It!

Every day, you observe. If you watch a sport being played, that's observation. If you watch your dog catch a ball, that's observation. If you watch grass grow or paint dry, you are observing. If you watch your dad bake a cake or your mom wash the dishes, you are observing them, too. (Of course, you shouldn't just watch your mom and dad do chores. Ask them if they need some help! Good scientists are also very courteous.)

To observe things the way a scientist does, you must not only watch, but you must also eat a slice of pizza. Just kidding! I was checking to see if you were paying attention. That's because a good scientist not only watches but also PAYS ATTENTION. Get it? To observe like a scientist is to watch and pay attention.

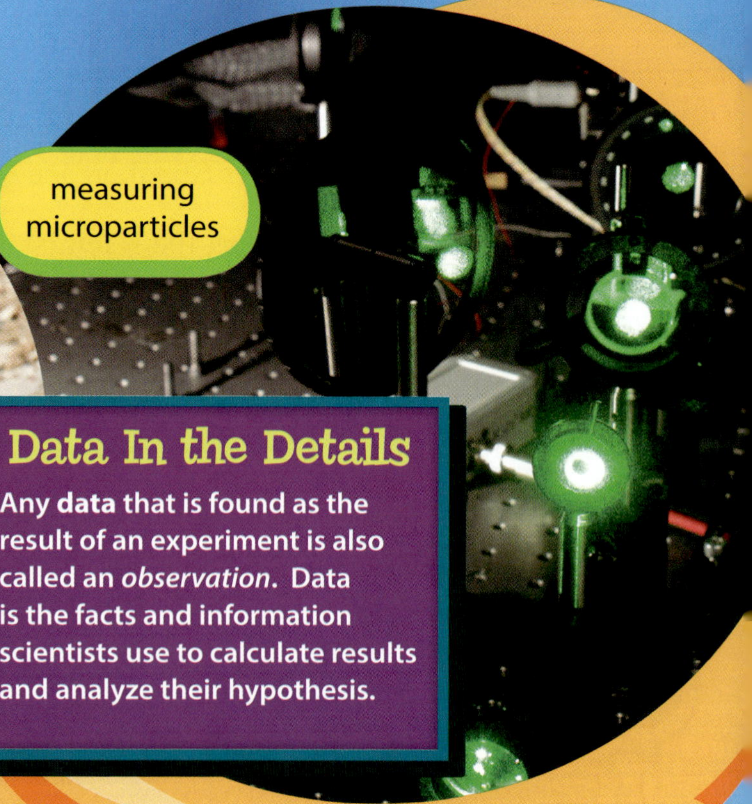

measuring microparticles

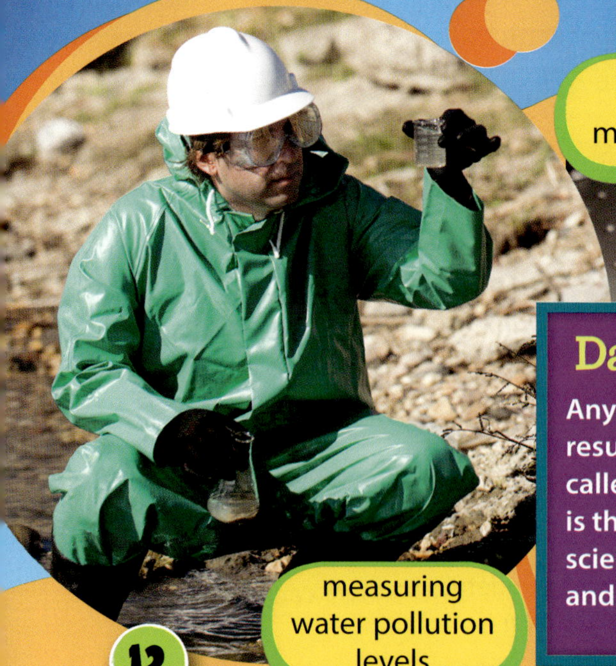

measuring water pollution levels

Data In the Details

Any **data** that is found as the result of an experiment is also called an *observation*. Data is the facts and information scientists use to calculate results and analyze their hypothesis.

A scientist really notices things. You do this with your eyes, of course. You see things, and you think about what you see. You also observe like a scientist when you use your nose and ears. You smell odors and you hear sounds. You smell and hear them change, as well. And, if it's safe to do so, you can also use your hands and tongue to observe. You touch things and you taste things. You think about how things feel and how they taste. Your senses can tell you a lot. They might even tell the whole story if you really pay attention.

petri dish

compass

microscope

The ways you can observe with just your senses are almost endless! But your senses alone are not the only way to observe *scientifically*. There's a lot in the world that can't be observed with your senses alone. Can your eyes see individual light waves? Can your ears hear a flea crawling on a dog? Can you feel the difference between your DNA and a geranium's? No!

Scientists are a pretty smart group of folks. They've developed tools to help them do their jobs. The tools enhance, or improve, what the senses can do. They might make things bigger or brighter so they can be seen. They can also do what the senses can't do! For example, we can't just feel something to know its weight. Well, maybe we can make a pretty good guess! But we really need a scale to give us the exact measure.

Scientific tools don't need to be fancy, although some are. Some of the best tools are really the simplest ones.

Tools of the Trade

Some of the most common tools used by scientists include microscopes, telescopes, thermometers, rulers, scales, cameras, clocks, barometers, binoculars, and tape measures. What other tools can you think of?

telescope

Patterns

What exactly does a scientist look for when observing? It really could be anything. So, a scientist observes with something in mind to focus his work. For example, if he wants to know about the effects of moonlight on sunflowers, he's going to observe—you guessed it!—moonlight on sunflowers. Sounds pretty simple, right?

A scientist will notice everything and make note of it. Part of that "noticing" includes looking for patterns in what he observes. Patterns are sequences that repeat. They may reveal something important. The moon follows a pattern of phases. Sunflowers have a pattern of florets in their centers.

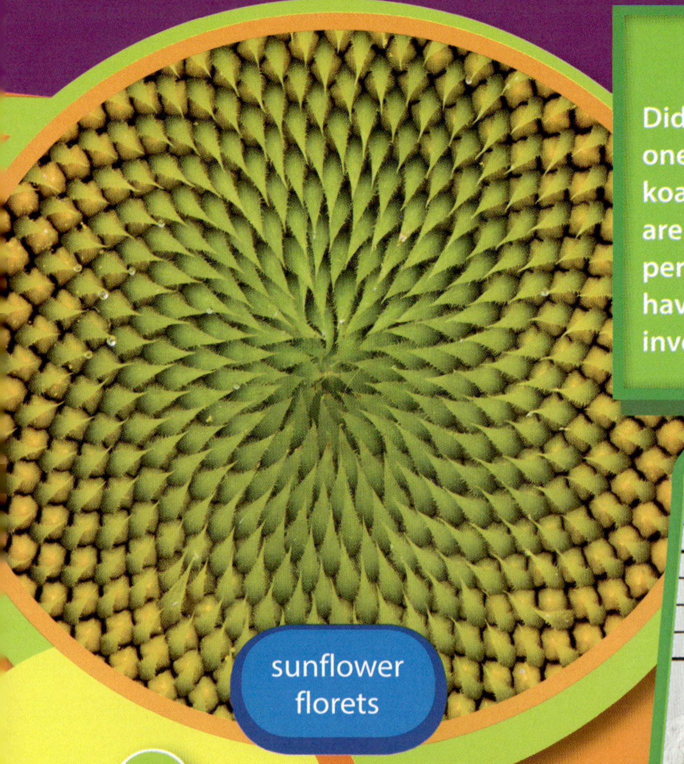
sunflower florets

Fingerprints

Did you know that humans aren't the only ones with fingerprints? Primates and koalas have fingerprints, too. Fingerprints are a pattern of swirls on fingertips. Every person's fingerprints are unique. Koalas have prints that look so human a criminal investigator can be fooled!

Looking for patterns also means noticing when something is a lot like something else that is not related to it. “Where have I seen that before?” the scientist might ask.

Take a look at the photos on this page of the owl and owl butterfly. The design pattern on the butterfly looks a lot like the eyes of the owl. Cool, huh? How did that happen, and why do you think it is? A scientist would use this pattern of observation to dig in further and find out.

owl butterfly

horned owl

sea anemone

violet anemone

Comparisons

Looking at patterns can lead to **comparisons**. For example, flowers called *violet anemones* look an awful lot like animals called *sea anemones*. Just look at the pictures, and you can make many comparisons. "Size! Shape! Cluster!" But a good scientist will study the real things closely to compare everything. She'll even compare how they're different. "Plant or animal? Air or water?" Then, the scientist will work to find out WHY they are similar and what that means. Scientists are very big on asking why. They are a curious group of people! In fact, curiosity in scientists is a definite pattern. Just compare them, and you'll find out for yourself.

Scientists also use comparison to study and analyze data. Data can help prove or disprove a hypothesis. Data helps scientists answer questions.

Constants

When conducting an experiment that uses comparison, scientists maintain a constant. A constant is something that doesn't change from experiment to experiment. Things being compared have to be tested against something that's the same—or constant—for both of them. Otherwise, there is no comparison!

Three seeds from the same parent plant were covered with dirt and placed in sunlight.

By using the seeds from the same parent plant and by placing all three plants in the sun, a constant has been created. This makes it easier to see the effect of different watering practices.

Data Collection

Observations are interesting, sure. But other than that, what's the big deal? Observations are actually a VERY big deal. Data comes from observations, and data is a scientist's bread and butter. Without data, a scientist is just a guy or a gal in a chair watching the world go by.

Data is the information that a scientist gathers from observations. Observations result in data. Data is gathered from activities of the senses. It's taken from tools and their readings. It's also collected as the result of experiments.

A scientist keeps good records of all this data. When it's gathered, the scientist looks it over and studies it. She analyzes what it means. She interprets it to see how it supports or refutes the hypothesis. Or maybe the data gives the scientist a whole new idea. It just may be time to start experimenting again!

A scientist carefully measures a liquid.

Get Organized!

Be sure to keep your data together in one place, whether it's a notebook or a computer. You can't analyze data if it's on sticky notes in your cat's litter box!

Students gather data from an experiment.

Tell It!

So, now that you've observed, hypothesized, predicted, and tested, what do you, oh scientist, do now? You've got to tell others what you've learned, what you've done, and what the evidence bears out. You could, of course, just keep it to yourself. But where's the fun in that? A scientist wants to know…and a *good* scientist knows that everyone benefits when information is shared.

It's like this: the understanding of science builds on itself. What one scientist learns becomes the basis for another scientist's investigations. And those investigations support other scientists. The work grows and grows. More is learned, validated, or even disputed. There's always more to discover and uncover. There's always more to know!

Scientists take measurements of a solar furnace.

Scientists have worked like a team throughout history. The work of scientists from the earliest recorded times carries forward to today. Today's work will carry forward through the future. Scientists come and go. What they learn lives on.

Long-Term Learning

Learning *why* something happens can take time. Some experiments take hundreds of years to complete! A *longitudinal* (lon-ji-TOOD-n-l) *study* is one that takes place over long periods of time. Researchers observe the same **variables** many times, looking for what stays the same and what changes.

It comes down to this: a scientist must be able to communicate findings to others. The information must be clear, organized, and precise. It also needs to be easily understood.

Take, for example, Newton's first law of motion, which is a basic scientific truth. It states that "an object at rest stays at rest and an object in motion stays in motion with the same speed and in the same direction unless acted upon by an unbalanced force." That's a mouthful! But what does it mean? It's not hard to understand, but it can be tricky to explain. What it means, simply stated, is that an object keeps doing exactly what it's doing unless something comes along to change it.

Let's put it into practice. Say you're riding a skateboard. You're going along full steam ahead. Suddenly, there's a rock in your path, and you don't see it. Bam! The rock stops the skateboard dead in its tracks. But you keep sailing forward…until gravity forces you down and an unfriendly sidewalk smacks you. (Safety tip: Always wear a helmet and pads, my friend!)

A scientist can use the skateboard story to help explain Newton's first law. You understand it now, don't you? A good story always helps to make things clear!

Keep It Simple

Occam's razor is an idea that says the simplest hypothesis is often the best hypothesis. Sometimes, a question requires a complicated answer, but when you don't have a lot of time or information, it makes sense to trust the simplest answer first.

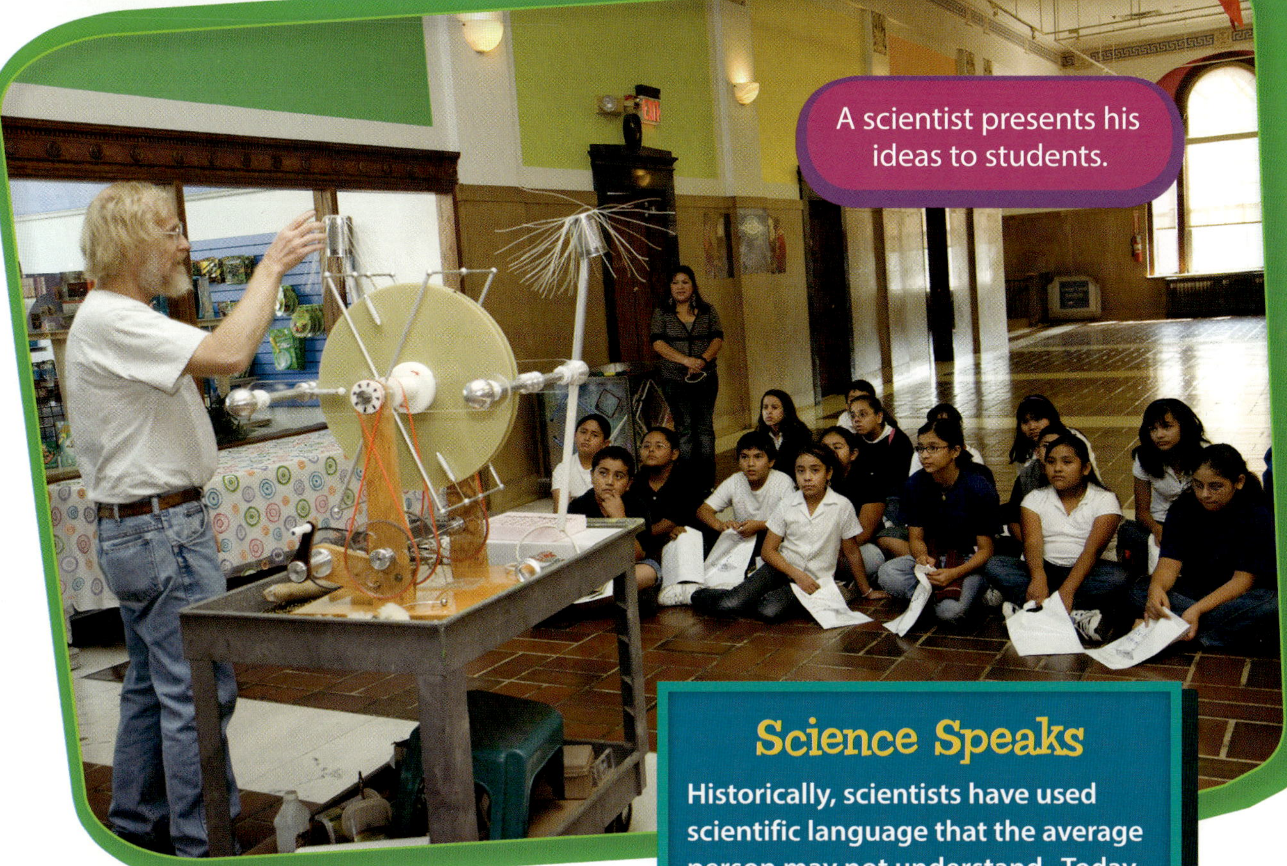

A scientist presents his ideas to students.

Science Speaks

Historically, scientists have used scientific language that the average person may not understand. Today, there are classes to teach scientists how to communicate with everyone. Some scientists are even learning improv to appeal to the masses!

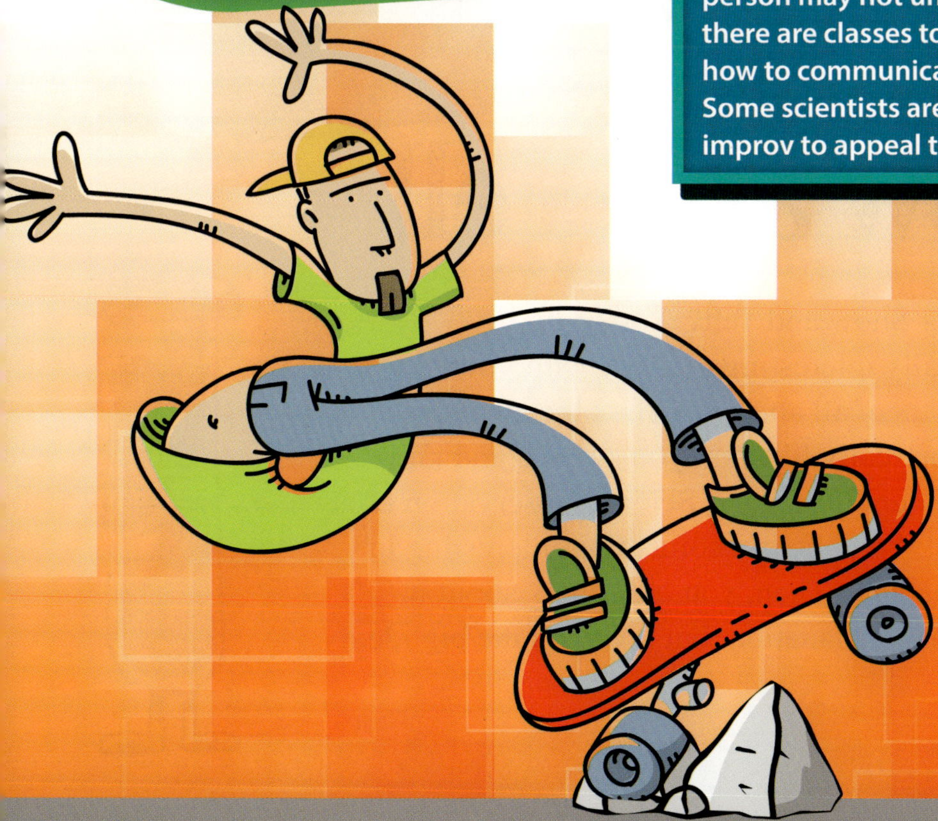

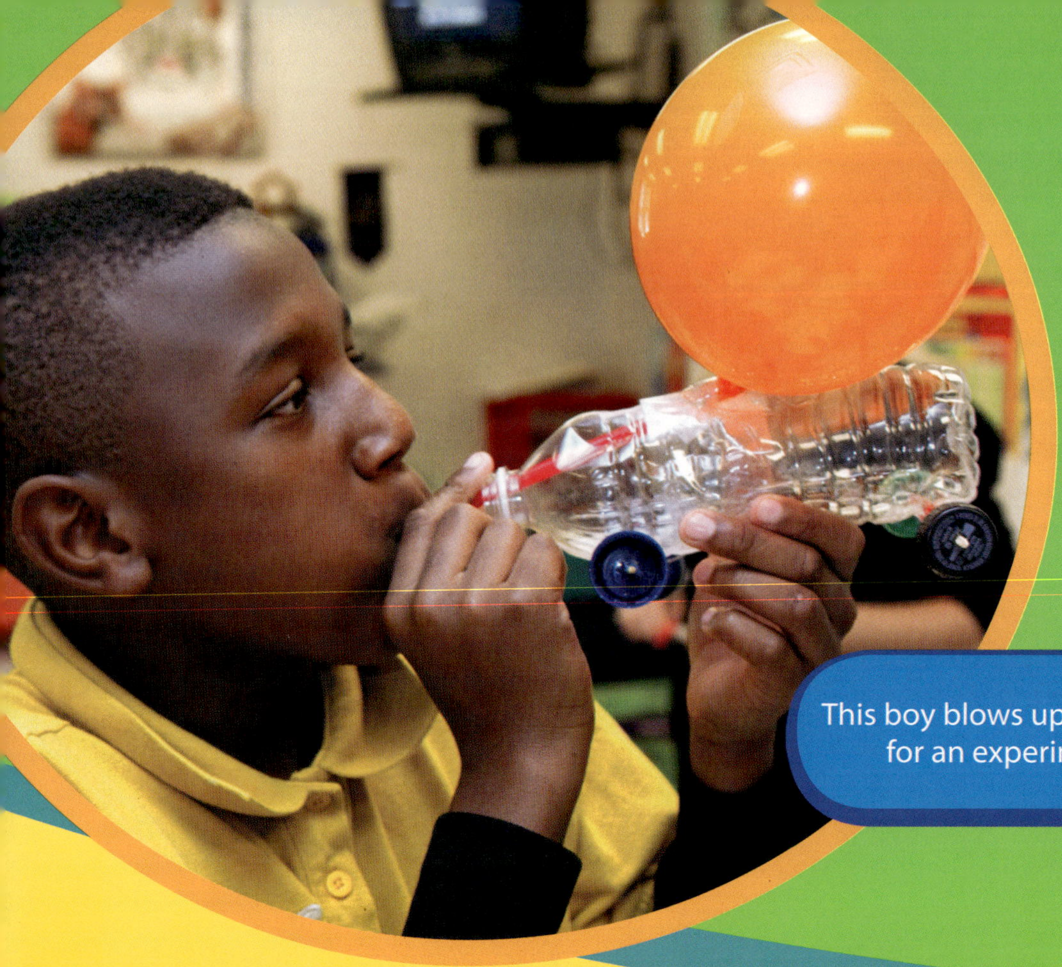

This boy blows up a balloon for an experiment.

Show and Tell

Remember Show and Tell? You bring in something really interesting to share with your class and tell them all about it. The object can be something you really like that you studied and know a lot about. Sound familiar? Science observation is a lot like that! You observe something interesting in every way you can. Then, you tell others about it. That's a simple explanation, but it covers the big idea!

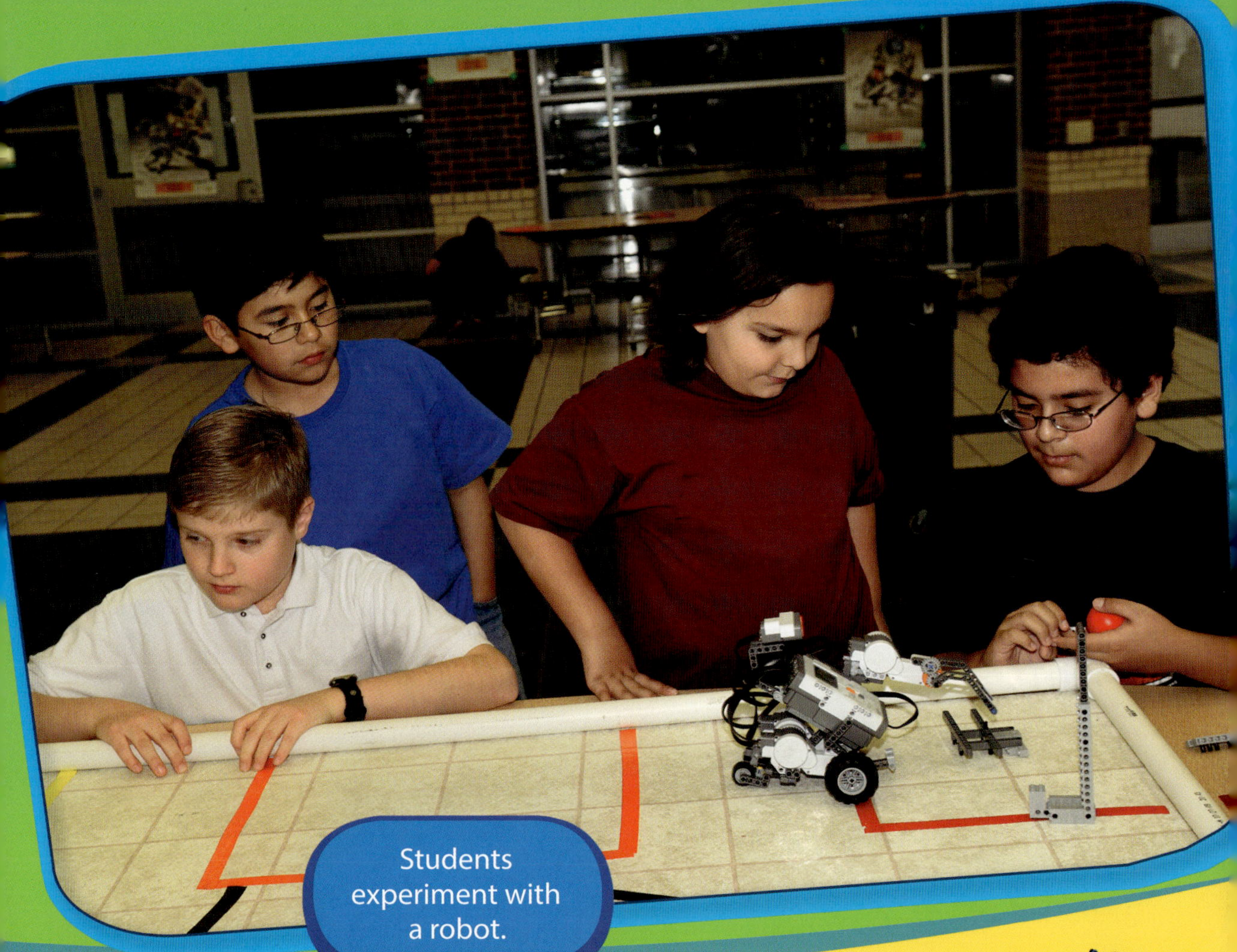

Students experiment with a robot.

Science is really about letting your curiosity take over and learning all you can about something you find really interesting. How does it work? What does it do? What happens if…? These are all great questions!

So, it's time to get our your magnifying glass out and get ready to observe the world around you. Just be careful where you put your tuna fish sandwich!

Think Like a Scientist

How can a magnifying glass help you observe the world? Experiment and find out!

What to Get

- clear, thin plastic container
- craft knife
- plastic wrap
- rubber band
- small items
- 5 centimeters x 15 cm (2 inches x 6 in.) strip of sturdy cardboard
- water

What to Do

1. Cut a rectangular hole near the bottom of the side of the plastic container. The rectangular hole should be about 7 cm (3 in.) wide and 5 cm (2 in.) tall. (An adult should do this!)

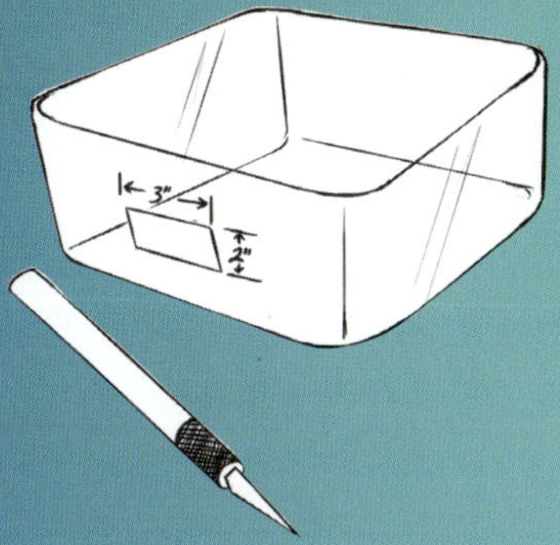

2. Place the plastic wrap over the top of the container, leaving the newly cut hole free and clear. Push the wrap into the center of the container a bit to make a little depression.

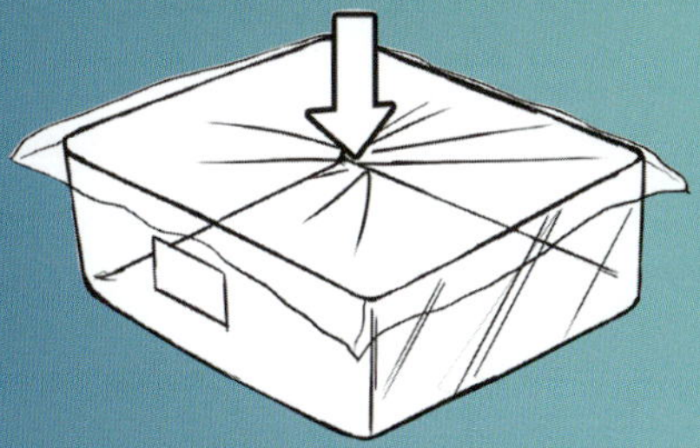

3. Secure the plastic wrap with a rubber band. Pour some water into the plastic wrap.

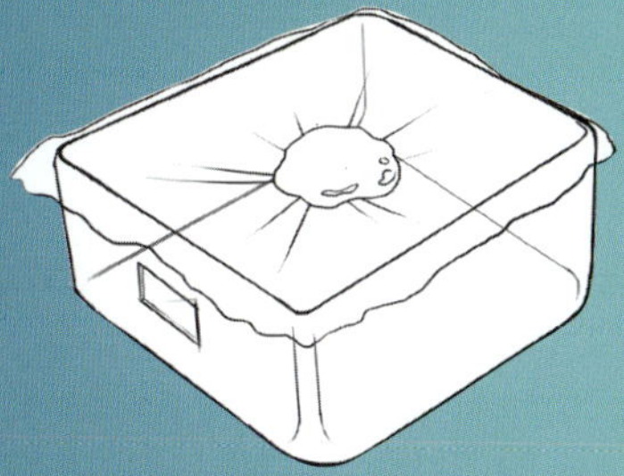

4. Place an item to be magnified on the short edge of the cardboard. Slide it through the hole in the container under the water. What do you notice? How might this be a useful tool?

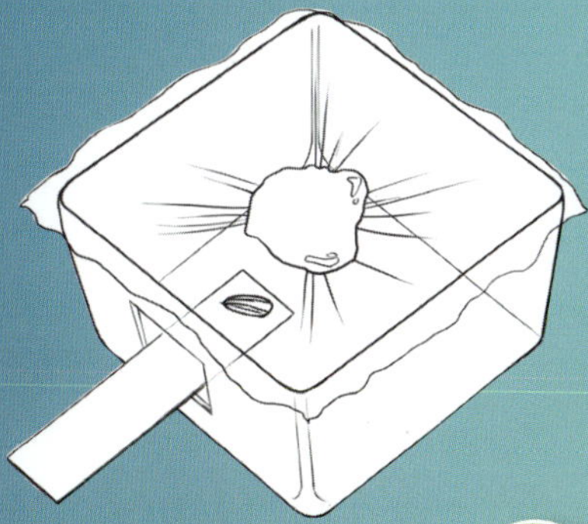

Glossary

analyzes—studies something to learn about its parts, what it does, and how it relates to other things

chemicals—substances made when atoms or molecules change

comparisons—acts of looking at things to see how they are similar or different

conducting—doing

data—information used to calculate, analyze, or plan something

equal—the same

hypothesis—an idea that is not proven and needs to be studied further

observation—the act of carefully watching and listening

prediction—an educated guess based on the information you know

research—to collect information about something

scientific method—steps used by scientists to test ideas through experiments and observation

valid—true and proven

variables—things that change or that can be changed

Index

Your Turn!

Look Closely

With an adult's help, light a candle and observe what happens. What do you notice about the flame? About the candle? About the air around it? Write every detail that you observe.